UP YOUR INCOME

UP YOUR INCOME

Create A Second Income Without
Getting A Second Job!

Ladimer Kowalchuk

DEDICATION

To my family who has stuck by me through all of my
crazy adventures, some of which worked out and
some of which didn't.

CONTENTS

INTRODUCTION

The advent of the television shows "American Pickers", "Storage Wars", as well as "Pawn Stars" has been instrumental in making people aware of the tremendous opportunities that are out there just waiting to be picked. Not only can it be profitable, but it can also be a lot of fun as an individual or as a family/group venture. It would be hard, if not impossible for the average person to duplicate the "American Pickers", "Storage Wars" successes. Although entertaining; it is not practical to buy a van and run around the country trying to pick a bargain. The guys on "American Pickers" work way too hard. There is a much better, easier way to do this in your home area without all of the complications associated with life on the road.

It is possible to replace your day job!

I can make that statement with confidence! I have lived every part of what I am going to show you.

My name is Ladimer Kowalchuk. I wrote *Up Your Income* in order to share my methods with as many people as possible.

The book is based on my life experience in the game of buying and selling. There are many people in the world that buy and sell, there are also many books on buying and selling.

My "claim to fame" is that I have bought and sold virtually everything from bicycles, to horses, to businesses, to airplanes (later in the book I share a list of some of the things I have bought and sold). I am a grade nine graduate. I'm not a financial guru. I have developed a system that allows me to virtually buy and sell at will in almost any market. I have learned many tricks over the years which I intend to share with you. I will also share some of my mistakes. The system is surprisingly simple and easy to follow.

In the early years I had no funds and had to use my wits to get things done. I did all of this while living in a small town with a population of less than 1,000 people.

When you first start out it can be difficult to get funding so you have to be creative. **In this book I will show how to get inventory for free or almost free.**

I will explain how to get started with little or no money. If you are interested in having a better more profitable lifestyle; this book is for you.

"It's so easy, even a caveman can do it!" (Sorry, I just had to use that line because bartering is truly as old as man himself.) It took 40 years to perfect my system into something I could consistently teach others.

I have always been driven to make extra money, not by greed but by the desire to have things that my regular income could not give me. My system for buying, selling, and trading will work for anyone who applies it.

I am literally going to show how you can begin with a few dollars, in some cases no cash at all, to start a lucrative/profitable buy/sell career.

"But…!" you say. "I have never sold anything in my life!" Wrong! If you have a job you are selling your time to your employer. Your time is sold in the form of labor or knowledge or both. In many cases you are selling your time for next to nothing. This book will show you how to drastically increase your time/value ratio.

There is no better or fun way on this planet of increasing your income. I still get a rush when I sell for a profit!

Things you shouldn't worry about:

- **Don't worry about how to get started.** By the time you have read this book you will know all there is to the buy/sell/barter game. You will learn methods that will become a part of your daily routine.

- **Don't worry about where you live.** I live in a small town with less than 1,000 people. Thanks to the internet, boundaries don't matter.

- **Don't worry about having a lot of cash to spend.** I will show you how to get started with little, or even, no money.

- **Don't worry about your age.** My 12 year old grandson made $1100 on his first deal. (Admittedly I had something to do with it. I lent him the funds to get started, and I showed him how to make a buy that earned him his first profit.) Think he will do it again? He already has. Once you get started and do a couple of successful deals you'll be hooked.

3

- **Don't worry about what you are going to buy, sell, or trade.** I will show that you are surrounded by items that you can buy and sell, many of them can be obtained for free or almost free. Most of us trip over more than $100 in a day.

- **Don't worry about the economy.** A poor economy will actually work in your favor.

- **...and don't worry about doing this alone.** Our "Pickers Club" on Facebook is designed to provide you the encouragement and guidance you need to confidently proceed; it is a fun place to share your winning stories, and learn from others as well! You can request to join the group for free at www.facebook.com/groups/pickersclub

This is not a get rich quick scheme. It is a wealth-building system that requires work and dedication. If you are lazy, please don't go any further. If you figure the world owes you a living; please don't go any further. If you're ready to roll up your sleeves and start picking and or trading with us...keep reading.

Don't read this book just for yourself. I helped my grandson with his first deal. He bought this car for $500, cleaned it up and sold for it $1600. He was 12 at the time

CHAPTER 1

THE MOST IMPORTANT THING YOU'LL NEED

There is one thing you need to have before anything else in order to get started. It is more important than money, things to sell or even time. When you have this, everything else will follow. That one thing is **commitment**. Commitment to the program; commitment to yourself; commitment to invest some time; commitment to let the money build. Commitment to be patient.

Throughout this book I will give several real scenarios to illustrate deals that I have done. I will use these deals to illustrate the steps I took to:

- Find the item.
- Determine what I would pay for the item.
- Price the item.
- Sell the item.

I will describe each of these steps along the way using real-life examples of what I did and how I did it. Just remember, some of these deals are dated and that under no circumstances should you use the prices as a guide to determine the present value of similar items. It is important to determine an accurate value and don't worry, I will show you several methods on how to do so.

Let's begin by putting something into perspective. This book is written to show anyone, young or old, how they can start buying and selling whether they have funds or not. Some of the examples I am going to give in this book may seem trivial if you already have a nice balance in your bank account. But not everyone does. If I give an example of where you can make $70 you need to realize that to a large part of the population that equals a day's wage, where they have to commit 8 hours plus the cost and time to get back and forth to and from work.

If you earn $12 per hour and get paid for 8 hours
8 x 12 = $96. If you are in a 25% tax bracket this leaves you
with $72. Take off your cost of getting to and from work as
well as your other deductions and you are lucky to walk
away with $60.

A $70 profit for selling something you spent two hours on, all of a sudden doesn't seem so bad does it? What if you worked that day and did this as a sideline? Do you see how it can grow? Don't expect miracles when you first get started, but if you concentrate on growing your resources you could see some pretty quick results. If you sold a measly two items a week at $70 profit, multiplied by 52 weeks, you would add $7,280 to your nest egg. I call it "Doubling Down". In ten years you would be ahead by $72,800. Double that to four items and in 10 years you are ahead by a whopping $145,600. Just think how much you can make if you really ramp things up.

The system I am going to reveal to you is not cash specific. In other words it will work anywhere on the financial scale. Rich or poor if you want to find a fun way to make extra funds the methods I teach can work for you. It is actually more a way of life than a specific system. You will develop a mindset that will remain with you for life.

You can start with almost any amount, even nothing. But even if you are comfortable spending large amounts; it is best to start slowly and gain some experience before you go in whole hog. It is more important to invest a lot of time when you are first starting out. In the early stages too much cash can actually be a hindrance if you have a careless nature. There is a learning curve in the buy/sell game and it is best learned in small increments.

I have split this book into four sections:

Goods – This section discusses what you should buy and where to find it.

Markets – Here we discuss where you can sell all the incredible things you have found. Places like online auctions, websites, regular auctions, classifieds, and your front yard. The list is endless.

Promotion – I will show you how to sell or market the items you have bought.

Money Matters – In this section we will talk about all things dealing with the money aspect of your new business, including how to begin without any, getting credit, controlling inventory, costs of doing business, bookkeeping and most importantly how to price your items.

Keep in mind there will be some overlap, and some chapters may seem like they are out of order, but we will try our best not to lose you.

Ready to learn? Let's go!

The owner wanted this house moved off his property. I bought it for $6,000. I spent $3000 for new shingles and some cosmetic fixes and sold for $13,800.

GOODS

What to buy and where to find it.

CHAPTER 2

WHAT SHOULD YOU BUY?

The first question is how much money can you commit? If you don't have any cash, don't worry. I will show you how to get started without it. There will be a whole section on money including where and how you can get it if you need it.

Let's assume you have some cash. Don't throw it all in the pot and go whole hog. You need to first gain some experience because you can make costly mistakes if you don't know what you are doing. This is not a get rich quick scheme where you are going to make a million dollars over night. The examples given in this book are real life episodes that I have done, and they can easily be duplicated. Remember you have to be committed and patient.

The first thing to consider would be finding something that you are interested in and that you have some knowledge of. For example, if you are into playing musical instruments, start checking ads and searching the internet to see what is out there and what price people are asking for these items.

When you read the later chapter on "The Psychology of a Buyer and a Seller" you will see why there can be a large spread between the amounts you pay and how much you can sell for.

If you know something about antiques, you could try specializing in antiques. If cars are your love, by all means get into the car game. You will note that a lot of my references will be to the car game. This is because at least 60% of the stuff I have bought and sold has been related to the auto industry.

Working with something you are interested in at the beginning will make it a lot more fun.

You may need to try a few different items to find your niche. A lot of your success will depend on your location and what the population of the area is. In a later chapter I will talk about how one of the first things I started with was bicycles. This example will work great in a big city on a continuous basis but wouldn't be practical in a small town like mine. Always think about supply and demand. There is no bike auction (no supply) in my hometown and not enough people to buy (no demand).

If you have a hobby, it is possible that you could turn it into a business. For example, if you are artistic and can paint a pretty good picture - get some prints made and market them. If you don't have a clue how to market them, don't worry. By the time you are finished reading this book you will have identified several ways of presenting any product for sale.

If you do woodworking or other crafts, you have a product. All you have to do is make and market them. If you are mechanically inclined you can buy and sell fixer uppers (things in need of repair).

If you have a specific skill or knowledge that you can share; it is marketable. I am writing this book in order to sell information. I have knowledge that is of value to you. In this case I am going to show several ways to increase income. You are investing in my book because you see the potential to use the information to make extra income. I am giving you knowledge for money. People can and will gladly pay you for your knowledge. In many cases your knowledge can be a lot more valuable than you realize.

Knowledge is power and can translate into profit if used properly. You can find some great information and meet other like-minded people in our free Facebook Group for Pickers. It is a great way of sharing experiences and information on a wide variety of markets.
www.facebook.com/groups/PickersClub/

Timing is everything. I bought this mower in December for $150 when there was no grass to mow and sold it in June for $475 when people had lots of grass to mow.

CHAPTER 3

BUYER AND SELLER MIND READING SKILLS

The Psychology of the Seller

Everyone's mind functions in basically the same way. A seller wants or needs to dispose of the article he is trying to sell. There could be several reasons for wanting to sell, trade, or give away an item. If you can figure out the seller's motivation you will be in a better position to negotiate a lower price. Remember, your money is always made when you buy. If a person is emotionally attached it will be difficult to get him to move on his price. Fortunately most of the time they just want to get rid of the article.

Don't worry about the asking price. If the item has been for sale for a while, the seller will already have lowered the value in his mind. Everyone has a wish price. Many times I have put a price on something and sold it for a lot less, especially if it has been around for a while.

Most people are uncomfortable advertising and selling items. This is why most people trade in their cars when they know they could get more by advertising and selling it privately. They just don't want to bother. To them, their old car/bike/furniture/appliance is just something to be gotten rid of.

This is why you see perfectly good items out on the curb, they didn't want to be bothered trying to sell it. People will throw away items that, in some cases, are worth several hundred dollars. I have seen furniture, appliances, cabinets, bicycles, barbeques, computers, and many other valuable items out on the curb for anyone to pick up.

There is an old saying: "Difference of opinion is what makes horse trading."

By understanding the difference in how the mind of most buyers and sellers works you will easily understand why there can be such a big spread between how much you buy something for and how much you can sell something for.

Most sellers don't have a clue as to what something is worth. I once bought a $55,000 gravel truck for $35,000 on eBay. I search eBay, on a regular basis. The truck was a new listing with a "Buy It Now" of $35,000. It had low miles and was in almost new condition. I hit the "Buy It Now" button and I was the proud owner. There had only been ten views at the time. (It had only been listed for about 4 hours). I could have fooled around bidding on it and tried to get it for less, but I pulled the trigger instantly. I buy and sell gravel trucks and knew that the truck was way underpriced.

After the deal was done I was talking to the seller and asked him how he had come up with the price. He told me that they no longer needed the truck and had decided to downsize their fleet. Three of the business owners sat down and discussed how to sell the truck and how much to sell it for. They came to an agreement that if they put it on eBay and got $35,000 they would be satisfied. Of course, I asked if they had any more trucks that they wanted to get rid of. Unfortunately that was the only one.

What they should have done is check the market by calling a dealer, check what other similar trucks are listed for, check auction reports for pricing on similar items, check local ads, etc.

If they had called a dealer and asked him to make an offer they would have easily gotten more for the truck. They left between $10,000 and $20,000 on the table. This is not an isolated situation, it happens all the time. If you know the value of a certain product and search eBay regularly you will find similar opportunities. The trick is to know your value and to know when to pull the trigger. Their loss is your gain.

Sellers are basically motivated by several different situations; the best one is "need".

They *need* the room, they *need* the money, they *need* to replace the item with a newer better bigger item, they are moving, they no longer have any use for the item, divorce, settle an estate, lost a contract, going out of business, I could go on and on.

The "Need Seller" is usually the easiest to buy from because he is in a position where he has to dispose of the item and the bigger hurry he is in the better. No matter what the asking price, don't be afraid to make an offer at the price you would be comfortable with. If they turn down your offer, leave them your number and tell them to let you know if they change their mind. Or, if you know your values and know you can pay more, make a counter offer. It is usually smartest to put a time line on your offer, this will create a sense of urgency for them to make up their mind. When given a deadline we all tend to work toward it.

Never leave your offer open for more than a few days. At the end of the time line, don't be afraid to call and ask if they are ready to take your offer. In a lot of cases they will have given up on selling the item and if you catch them at the right time you're likely to hear, "To hell with it. Come and get it."

I live in Canada in the summer and in Florida in the winter. One spring, on one of our walks in a marina with a mobile home park, I saw a waterfront doublewide mobile home with a "For Sale" sign on it. We walked by it regularly and the sign had been up all winter. I said to my wife, "The selling season is at an end, let's check this out." (My mindset is to always be looking for opportunity.)

The owner was asking $29,900. I thought this was reasonable for waterfront so I called the number and asked to see the place. They had it rented and were not interested in anyone seeing the place. It took a couple of days of persistence before we finally got in to see it. (Persistence is a good trait when you are buying and an even better one when you are selling).

We noted that it needed more work inside than we had anticipated. We talked to the renter and asked if he planned on staying or was thinking of moving. He said he definitely did not want to move. This added value to me because of the $550 lot rent. This is an upper scale gated 55+ park in a marina (that is why the rent is so expensive).

I estimated it would take $5,000-$10,000 to make it nice. I offered $10,000 for it, after pointing out that it needed work. It was obvious that the owner had no interest in keeping it up. The owner countered at $15,000 and we made a deal. You will notice that I paid half of what he was asking. His comment was that he knew it was worth a lot more but he just wanted to get rid of it. I still own it at the time of this writing - 36 months later. My renter wants to stay so I am going to let him pay its way for another couple of years or so. The market is coming back up in price and by holding it for a while I will make a lot more money.

When I sell, I will have spent about an additional $10,000. With the proper presentation it will easily get a lot more than the $29,900 that the original owner was seeking. I think with the proper ad at the high time of the season, I could get $55,000+ without doing the renovations. I will give an example that will show you how it can be done.

The seller's mistakes were:

- He didn't fix it up for sale. (Detail for retail.)
- He didn't market it properly. A small sign on the outside wall was all he had.
- He didn't have the co-operation of the renter. He told the renter he was going to kick him out on short notice if he sold.
- He didn't even have the grass cut.

His poor presentation actually worked against him.

What I would have done if it were mine and I was selling it in the condition it was in:

- I would have marketed it as a fixer upper which is what it is
- I would cut the grass
- I would have placed ads worded something like this example...

Waterfront mobile home for sale!!!
Once in a lifetime opportunity to live on the water! This home is located in Saint Petersburg's Bay Pines Marina, one of the nicest, most secure gated 55 plus parks in Florida. The Marina has boat access to John's Pass and the Gulf of Mexico. It is a 2 bedroom 2 bath home with all of the amenities. The interior is livable but is dated and in need of some renovations, the exterior is very nice. Walk out your front door onto the boat dock. Pictures available at www.xxxxxxxxx.com Please call for appointment 727 xxx xxxx. Priced at only $59,900 OBO.

I would post on local sites like Craigslist with links to the Bay Pines Marina website as well as the Harbor Lights Club website. I would list more features that make this one of the most desirable parks in all of Florida, (which it is), such as the connection to the Pinellas trail and the Veterans Memorial Park. I would tell them that they have boat access right from their front door to John's Pass as well as the Gulf of Mexico. I would put links to both the Pinellas Trail and the Veteran's Memorial Park on the site to make it easy for people to check everything out. I would encourage them to look it up on Google Earth to see the location with all of the water around it.

If you aren't computer savvy you can easily get someone else to post it for you for a few bucks. I don't do my own listings and have no desire to learn how. I get a friend that is up on computers to do my ads.

Do you see where I am going with this?

I'm not just selling the mobile home, I am selling a very desirable way of life in the nicest mobile home park in Florida that you can buy for not a lot of money. It is all about the presentation. I wouldn't just put in a humdrum ad that says "Mobile Home For Sale".

A buyer that is looking for a mobile home and does the research I have offered him will pay a lot more for my home than he will for one located in a park he knows a lot less about. The only thing that might kill their interest is if they are looking for a pristine ready to move into place. I could offer to sell it with the renovations by getting a quote before listing it and offering it either way.

The Psychology of the Buyer

It is important to understand the way buyers think too. All buyers tend to be similar in their pattern of how they approach the seller.

Here is a typical scenario:

A buyer pulls into your driveway to look at the car you have for sale. He walks around looking for flaws. If you have done things correctly you will have told him or sent him pictures showing any major flaws. Don't apologize for flaws, all vehicles have some. If you try to hide them you are just leaving the negotiating power in the buyer's hands because he can say, "Hey you didn't tell me about this dent. How much are you going to deduct for it?" If you tell him the truth ahead of time, it is no longer an issue or a bargaining point.

In the buyer's mind he will feel the need to lower the value by picking it apart. He will try to point out flaws to try to get the value down in your mind. If he shows you a minor flaw, don't go apologizing all over the place. Instead, say, "Yeah I noticed a couple more flaws…" and point them out to him too. Tell him that is why you put such a modest price on it. This lets him know that they aren't important and can't be used as a bargaining chip.

Expect the buyer to try to devalue your product – it's a natural thing. You will find yourself doing it when you are buying.

Expect to be offered less than your asking price. We just can't help ourselves, we need to feel that we got the best deal, the lowest price possible. Buying for a bargain price is almost as big of a rush as selling for a good profit.

Tip: Always price your product with some wiggle room on the price. Most people have a mental block against paying full price and won't pay it no matter what. By letting them win, you win.

In the same breath never ever accept a buyer's first offer. Let's say you are selling your neighbor's boat. He has had it sitting around for a long time and you have asked him if he wants to get rid of it. He says he doesn't know what it's worth, but if you get him $1000 for it, he will let it go. You put it online, put it in the local paper, post a picture and a write up on a local billboard, clean the boat up, and park it by a high traffic street.

Along comes your first buyer. You have done your homework and know that similar boats sell for between $1500 and $2000. You have advertised the boat for $1900 and know that this is probably the nicest boat they will find in the price range. The buyer brings an "expert" friend (I hate experts, they have a need to prove they are an expert and will try extra hard to show their knowledge). I turn those situations around by highlighting the finer points and asking him/her to acknowledge them.

Example: "The upholstery sure is nice for a boat this old, isn't it George?" He has to agree although he hates to do it. I just attempt to show more positives than he can negatives. It's almost a fun little game.

Back to our example. Let's say he offered you $1500. You could take it and walk away with a tidy profit, but… if he offers $1500 - 9 times out of 10 he will pay more. If you immediately accept his offer, he will think "Ah crap!! I could have gotten it for less."

Remember he needs to think he won, not that he over paid. Usually when I make a low-ball offer it is to try to get the seller to lower the value in his mind. I expect him to ask me for more. I am basically fishing for the lowest possible price. A lot of times if they just want to get rid of it they will take my offer. Always ask for more. The buyer can say no but a lot of times this will be a bluff.

Once you have asked him for more money, change the subject so that he feels pressured into making the next move. If he is walking on you, there are two things you can do. One is to tell him that if it isn't sold in the next week, you will call him. If he genuinely wants it, he won't take the chance that it will get sold to someone else. Second is to say "You can have it" at that price or say, "OK, you win". I will take your offer

Never ever lie and say you have another buyer. When people tell me this I ask them why they are wasting their time with me if they already have a buyer. Basically, by saying this you are creating a challenge (either you buy it from me or I will sell it to the other guy). When you challenge people they usually react negatively. No one wins.

CHAPTER 4

OBVIOUS AND NOT-SO-OBVIOUS PLACES TO FIND GOOD STUFF

You are literally surrounded by items you can buy and sell. Once you have finished reading this book you will become aware of opportunities that you didn't know existed. You will train your mind to always look for opportunity. You will develop a subconscious awareness.

If you take a drive around a ten square block area in your neighborhood, in most cases you will see one or two opportunities. Go into a different neighborhood and you will see similar opportunities as well as some new ones. Here are some obvious and not so obvious places to look:

Watch Store Ads for Closeouts

The other day a local department store sold off their shoes at two dollars a pair. New shoes for $2? How hard would it be to triple your money if you bought 100 pairs for $200? If you weren't interested in marketing them yourself you could go to a flea market and find two or three booths that sell shoes or similar items and get them to give you an offer or consign them for sale with their own stuff. Sell them on eBay or on local used good sites. Yes some people do sell new items on used item sites. The type of people that look on used sites are looking for a bargain. They will appreciate buying new for the price of used.

Check the Curb

Many times things are put out on the curb to be given away. Yesterday my neighbor put out a perfectly good barbeque. It was gone in a heartbeat. If he had put it on his lawn for $30 or $40. It would have still gone away, and he would be that much richer. You will find better stuff in an affluent neighborhood.

Check the Yard

If you see an old car sitting in someone's backyard, stop and ask them if they want to get rid of it. In a lot of cases they will give it to you for taking it away. If it doesn't run look in the paper or the yellow pages for a recycler that will pay you something to haul it away. Here are two ads I saw in the Saint Petersburg paper over the weekend: "We buy junk cars with or without title. $275 cash same day, anywhere 24/7." And, "Junk cars/$400 and up for junk or unwanted cars, trucks & vans. Same day service. Honest, fast service."

If it does run you may be able to take it home, clean it up, and sell it for a few hundred dollars more than the salvage price. If it is newer and he/she wants more for it than you have or are willing to give, ask him if you can try selling it for him. Be sure you research your values. Also be sure to have the right documentation and have a written agreement to prevent future problems. If the seller wants an unrealistic amount don't waste your time. List it on Craigslist and any other free local site. Use the same methods I showed you for just about anything, bikes, lawnmowers, furniture, you name it. I will show you many more marketing tricks throughout this book.

Do you see what I mean? There is no exact formula, but there is a mindset. Once you get this into your head you will be constantly on the hunt. Yes, it is like hunting. You never know when you will come across the next opportunity. The more aware and persistent you are the more successful you will be.

Watch for Super Sales

Every Thanksgiving, stores have a Black Friday sale. Last year, I saw Kmart sell a 50 inch television for $299. I'll bet if you bought one and advertised as a new, still in the box 50 inch television with warranty for only $499 in the used section of the paper you would probably find someone that would buy it. If you tried it and it didn't work out you could return it for a full refund (risk-free selling). In the present market we see these televisions sell in the $600 range. There are plenty of people that read the used ads that would never dream you could buy a new one for that kind of a price. A lot of times the used buyer will never even look at ads for new.

The used buyer has a mindset to buy used, this is what happened to me with a miter saw I talk about later. I made up my mind to buy a used one because I thought used would be cheaper. I assumed the flea market would be less and I didn't want to spend a lot for a saw I would only use once or twice.

Attend Auctions

One of my favorite places to buy is the auction. This is where things are taken for disposal. I have dedicated the next chapter to auction so I won't touch it here.

CHAPTER 5

AUCTIONS EXPOSED! HOW TO BID AND WIN AND WHAT TO AVOID

Auctions can be intimidating to anyone that is not familiar with them. I get about 45% of my product from auctions. I like them because usually they are product specific. In other words if I am looking for a bicycle I can go to an auction that has bikes for sale. Lumber, appliances, furniture, industrial supplies, real estate, antiques, collectors' items, rv's or automobiles, etc., - almost anything you could possibly want is readily available at auctions every day of the week, including Sunday. The auction machine never sleeps. Of course, the people or businesses that take stuff to an auction generally take it there because they want to get rid of it fast.

The auction world, once you understand it, can be a very good source – if not the best source – for finding things to buy and sell. If nothing else, it is the perfect place to go to learn your prices. I call it the real world of pricing. It is the only place

I know of that you can list something for sale and get more than you were asking for. It is the true supply and demand marketplace.

Example: You go to an estate auction and there is your regular run of the mill furniture, some antiques dishes, pictures, memorabilia, etc. In the garage is a stack of toolboxes. The old guy was a mechanic for 45 years. The majority of the crowd is there to buy the household stuff, if you are a buyer/seller or if you are interested in the tools for yourself, the scenario could unfold in two or three different ways. (Remember the supply and demand theory.) If you are the only one interested in the tools you are going to be getting one hell of a deal. If a few people want them they could go for a lot of money. There is only one way to find out and that is to set a price in your head and go for it.

In my mind a complete set of tools in a stacked toolbox on wheels would have cost the buyer thousands of dollars over the years. I personally would like to buy it for $500 or so. This set would be of interest to someone just starting out in the mechanic game. I would be willing to bet that if you called some technical schools that teach mechanics and told the instructor that you bought tools at an estate sale and want to resell them, that you would likely have a few buyers in a hurry. Also if you called the service managers of your local car dealerships they probably have someone starting out that needs tools and would be happy to let them know or post it on their bulletin board. Also trade specific magazines would be a good place to advertise.

You would want to have an itemized list as well as some pictures available to send prospective buyers. Also ask if they would post it on their bulletin board, and of course advertise in as many places as possible, especially the free ones. I suspect

I could ask $1400 for the set so I know getting it for $500 would be safe. Of course, a lot of buying is based on gut feeling, and a collection of items like this aren't easy to research, so it is possible that it could sell for a lot more. You'll have to rely on your gut instincts a lot at auctions.

Before You Go

Auctions make hunting for great finds easier because you can get a run list in advance (this is a numbered list of all of the items being sold in the sale). I always start by reviewing the list and putting a check mark next to the items I am interested in.

If it is a huge auction and there are a lot of potential items I am interested in, I may go the day before for viewing. Pretty much all auctions have a scheduled time that you can preview the items listed. Once I have marked my list, I will look at the items on the list and mark down what I am prepared to bid. There may be as many as 30 or 40 items or there may only be 1 or 2. I tend to put low-ball values on things that I am only passively interested in because at an auction; you never know when they are going to practically give something away. It happens all the time.

Learning the Auctioneer Lingo

One of the biggest hurdles to get over is understanding the auctioneer's chant. If you just sit back and listen for about twenty minutes, you'll quickly figure it out.

Basically he will start like this: "Here is some fine furniture. What are you going to give? Who will start me at $100?" Then he will add, "One hundred, give me one hundred, one hundred? Ok then fifty. I've got fifty now. I need a hundred..." At this time he may or may not have $50. At some point they need to get the bidding started. I usually don't bid until I see someone else bidding unless the price is ridiculously low. If he is chanting for $100 to start, don't be afraid to hold up ten fingers – indicating you're offering $10. They need to start somewhere.

In an Unreserved Auction, the auctioneer will start with any live money they get. Live money is a legitimate bid, not a ghost bid from the auctioneer. (A ghost bid is where the auctioneer does the bidding for the seller trying to get the bidding up to the amount the seller wants for the item.) In the next few sections I will explain the difference between reserved and unreserved auctions, buy backs, shill bidding, if bids, seller approved bids, online bidding, proxy bids and more.

Different Types of Auctions

There are basically three types of auctions: Unreserved, Reserved, and what I call B.S. Unreserved.

A truly Unreserved Auction will sell everything absolute to the highest bidder no matter what the price. This is usually the best auction to buy at because you know it is you and whoever else wants the item bidding and not the auctioneer running you up. The biggest legitimate auction I know of is Ritchie Brothers Auction. They are a worldwide publicly traded company and are run professionally with no games. They offer online bidding as well as onsite bidding. Their online bidding fees are reasonable (many auctions charge you a buyer's fee of up to 15%. This doesn't mean much on a $10 item but on a $10,000 item it is $1500 extra). This can take all of the fun out of the purchase as well as making it impossible to make any money.

Tip: A lot of auctions have buy fees for online as well as onsite auctions. They also charge extra for credit card transactions. You need to know how much they are and calculate them into your bid.

The second type of auction is Reserved Auction, where items can be sold with a set minimum. The seller brings the item to the auction and sets a minimum selling price for the auctioneer. If the bidding doesn't reach this price the auctioneer will either pass to the next item or he will do an "if" or phone bid. In this case the high bidder is expected to stay committed to the bid for an agreed amount of time. Sometimes it is an hour and sometimes it is until the end of the day or even longer. If you have limited funds and want to bid on another item coming up in the sale you can tell the auctioneer that you want off and don't want to do a phone bid. If you end up with nothing by the end of the sale you can always go into the office and reactivate the phone bid. Also a lot of times; if you go the next day and ask if they have a no sale list you can go around and see if there is anything that didn't sell that you might be interested in. This is a super good way of getting a bargain. If you get to know the auction staff, a lot of times they will give you insider info, such as, "That piece of equipment has been here for the last three sales. No one even bid on it in the last sale. It is a dead dog here."

A lot of times a seller will take less after the auction is over when he realizes the item is worth less than he thought. This could be a good time to make an offer. The staff will have a pretty good idea of what can be bought at a reduced price. This works well with Bank owned repossessions because a lot of times the bank can't make a decision on the day of the auction because more than one person may be involved in the decision. A well run auction is always working on getting things sold

The third type of auction is the B.S. Unreserved Auction. (I label it "B.S." because it's not truly what they say it is.) I don't like this type of auction because they aren't being honest with the buyers. How it works is the seller brings his item to the auction basically trolling it through trying to get it up to his selling price. This is done either by the auctioneer knowing his reserve and ghost bidding against you or the owner or his representative bidding against you. I have had many auctioneers say to me during their chant (It's just me and you buddy). This lets me know that he is running me. If I am comfortable with the price I will carry on anyway.

A good way to determine if it is a B.S. Unreserved Auction is to watch the inventory. If you are at a car auction and see a particular vehicle sell for X and then see it running through again the next week you can be pretty sure about the B.S.

Getting Help at the Auction

The term "ring man" stands for the two or three guys or gals in the ring trying to attract bids from the crowd. They assist the auctioneer in collecting bids. They will work you for the next bid by getting in your face and asking you to bid but they can also be a lot of help. If you have questions about what the auctioneer announced or if you don't understand where the bidding is at (some auctioneers are hard to understand), ask the ring man. It is their job to make sure you understand. Many times I will ask the ring man what the present bid is if I have any doubt at all. You should direct your bids to the ring man.

If you have made a bid and realize you made a mistake immediately let the ring man know that you made a mistake. He will let the auctioneer know that he needs to rebid the item. Be firm, they will try to keep you committed but if you made an honest mistake they will let you out.

The Proxy Bid

One of my favorite methods of bidding is called a Proxy Bid. Proxy Bids are bids you place in advance of the auction. They are used for both online auctions and live auctions. How they work is you place a bid that you are willing to pay for a certain item. Bids will then be placed on your behalf up to your maximum bid.

For example: I am online looking at government surplus disposal auction listings. There is a gravel truck and an office desk that I am interested in but the sale is on Wednesday and I am scheduled to be in meetings all day Wednesday. I want the truck and am willing to pay $15,000 for it. I am registered with a company that is actually called Proxibid - which submits bids on your behalf to auctions that use its service. I like Proxibid because I know it is legitimate. I know this auction charges a 10 percent buyer's fee, so I place my bid at $13,600. I also place a bid on the desk according to the price I am willing to pay. The day of the sale I am in my meeting and at 11:00 the gravel truck goes through the ring. Proxibid bids on my behalf and I end up owning the truck for $12,300!

Other Types of Bidding

I also use the proxy bid system for what I call Shotgun Bidding. Shotgun Bidding is basically peppering low-ball bids at a large number of items hoping that there are one or two that no one bids on. In many sales where they take bids or tenders on there can be certain items that no one bids on. This actually happens more often than you think. Throughout my many years of experience I have noticed that at every auction there is always an item that sells for a ridiculously low price. This is due to the supply and demand theory. The item is at the auction (supply), but there are no buyers (demand) for that particular item. On a proxy bid, if you low-ball a lot of items every once in a while you will win. A lot of times an item that has no value at one sale can bring a lot of money in another market. I'll tell you a short story with a lesson and then we will move on.

A couple of years ago a friend of mine was at a city disposal sale. He bought a miniature street sweeper for $1600 - one you ride on but not a great big one like you see sweeping city streets. It was like new and I guess the city had bought it and never used it. It only had about 150 hours on it and ran like a charm. He brought it home and put it in his garage.

I asked him what he was going to do with it. He said he might try to get some parking lots to sweep but that he just bought it because it was so ridiculously cheap. He asked me what I thought it was worth. I had no way of researching a price but I said, "If you wanted one, where would you look to find one?"

Long story short he advertised it for sale on line and in the Auto Trader and sold it for just over $10,000 to a guy that was looking for that exact size of machine to service a contract that he had available. Apparently a new one is quite expensive.

I bought this house new in 2013 at a disposal auction. I took out a mortgage and don't have a penny invested. It nets over $1000 per month in rent and its worth about $100,000 more than I paid for it.

For links to the most popular auction subscription sites, visit our *Up Your Income* resource page at **www.upyourincomeclub.com/resources**. Don't forget to join our Picker's Club Facebook group at: **www.fb.com/groups/pickersclub**. It's free!

CHAPTER 6

SHOTGUN BIDDING AND OTHER GREAT BUYING TIPS

Buying is all about being in the right place at the right time and then having the skill to pull off a fair deal. Pretty much 90% of your success is going to depend on your buying skills. I said "skills" because, as you get going, you will be constantly honing your buying skills. Truly your money is made when you buy. I probably spend an average of three or four hours a day searching for something to buy. Yes I am "hooked" on buying. I pretty much sell stuff just so I can go out and buy some more.

Typically I get up in the morning and check my e-mails. I am subscribed to at least 100 auctions. I get about 10 auction notices per day. These are mostly not local. They are scattered throughout the US and Canada. I will go over these and delete the ones that don't have anything I am interested in. The ones that have something of interest I will take a closer look at. If there is something of interest and the auction has a pre-bid or proxy option I will decide on a price I would like to pay and submit a bid. Then I will move on. You don't have to follow the item. The auction will let you know by e-mail if you won it or if you have been outbid. On a typical day I will throw bids at probably up to a dozen items. There is no emotion involved, it is just business.

I rarely get anything by using this method, but every once in a while "I win". I call this shotgun bidding. You obviously need to know your values before you throw bids at a lot of different items. This comes with time and experience. If you specialize in a certain field you can become knowledgeable fairly quickly. Make sure you know your values before you pull the trigger. If I find something that I am more than passively interested in, then I will pay more attention and bid with more emotion. I may also search other sites as well as auction history to determine a price I am comfortable with. (Many auctions publish a history report that shows past sales)

I like government disposal sites for a few reasons. One is variety, you never know what they will have listed. Two, they are almost always unreserved, you know that all bids against you are legitimate. Three, they will usually list the obvious flaws, such as the engine doesn't run or transmission is inoperable. They do not try to mislead anyone although in most cases everything is sold as is. I also like eBay, for both buying and selling; it is an open market place and one of the quickest ways to determine a value. Also you can get your product in front of a lot more people than you can locally.

On the *Up Your Income* Resource Page you will find links to all the auctions I subscribe to as well as more information on how to use them. There are also creative ways of finding certain products and receiving notices when they first show up online. One of these is Google Alerts. Visit the Free Resources page for details ay **www.upyourincomeclub.com/resources**

CHAPTER 7

INGENIOUS IDEAS FOR SELLING "WITHOUT" BUYING

Remember *I* said you don't always need money to start with? One of my favorite tricks is to have something sold before I buy it or even without buying it at all. This takes the risk out of the whole process. I have sold many things by using this method including a small business for $195,000. I made $9,750 putting the deal together. You may think you will never find a deal like that but it wasn't all that difficult.

The seller said to me, "I've had enough I need to get out." The buyer I knew was looking for an opportunity so I asked the seller if he would be willing to pay 5% if I could put a deal together. He told me he would gladly pay a fee if I could find a buyer. I got some preliminary information together and presented it to the buyer, the next thing I knew, the deal was on.

A few years back I noticed a handful of ads from people looking for a 345 International gas motor. This was in the 80's.

A lot of farmers had International trucks with the 345 engine. They were getting old and starting to fail. They were extremely hard to find. I stumbled onto this earlier when I bought a truck with a bad engine and had a hard time finding a replacement.

Once you get a mindset for buying and selling you begin to recognize opportunities that the average person would never see. I found a used auto parts store in a major city that had bought a whole fleet of retired school buses and dismantled them. He was marketing in his world where there was not much demand (the city). I advertised them in my world (the country 500 miles away). I sold every engine before I bought it by putting an ad in a farm paper. The long and short of the story is I sold the engines for an average of $1,800 each, plus freight. The wrecker was happy to get $1,000 each.

I would get paid up front before the engine shipped. Once I had the money in hand I would phone the wrecker and give him the shipping address and away it would go. I never, ever saw one of the engines. I had absolutely no investment other than the cost of the ad and I had zero risk. The wrecker even gave a warranty. I can't remember how many I sold but I know it was in the range of 20 or so in a two-year period. This is a prime example of how you can use someone else's inventory to your advantage.

Consignment

In a future chapter I'll talk about selling via consignment sales in more depth, but it's worth mentioning here now as a way to sell something without buying it first.

One quick example is finding a time sensitive product, like food, where a seller is motivated to have people helping him sell it quickly. You may be able to get a grower/vendor of produce to supply you with product. If he has an excess of produce he will probably be glad to consign it to you or to sell it to you at a deep discount instead of letting it spoil and throwing it away.

If you do not have the cash to buy the product and are honest with the vendor about your intentions, chances are he/she will give you a chance at selling their product. If you offer to pay at the end of every day, they won't have much risk. If you do make a deal to pay at the end of the day make sure to pay as per agreement or you will be out of business before you even get started.

Affiliate Marketing

If you are into marketing on the internet there is an endless supply of products to sell. This game is called affiliate marketing. How it works is you set up a website and advertise other people's products for them. The customer orders through their computer. The product creator collects the money and even handles the shipping. At the end of the month they send you a pre-agreed affiliate commission for any product sold through you. A lot of the products you see on the internet are sold using affiliate links. The opportunities are mind boggling.

There are several books and courses on this subject alone. You can find my current favorites on the Resources page as well. Some of them are free, and some are paid books and courses. Of course, if you order them through my links, I will also receive a commission and in some cases you may get bonus material too. See how the affiliate program works?

Now that we have found how we can get products to sell, let's talk about all the places we can sell them.

MARKETS

Finding the best places to sell your goods

CHAPTER 8

SELLING TO ANYONE ANYWHERE

Selling Online

The internet is the world's greatest marketplace. In one afternoon, you can register on multiple sites to sell almost anything anywhere. If you don't mind dealing with shipping costs, you can often get more money for your product by selling it to someone outside of your normal community. You can even take it to a local shipping company to package and ship the item for you (UPS offers these services in most areas). Just remember to add on a fee for shipping (and packaging). I'll discuss overhead costs in the next section.

Here's a list of prime online selling sites:

- eBay
- Amazon
- CraigsList (U.S.) or Kijiji (Canada)
- Newspaper Classified (pick your city)
- Facebook Buy/Sell/Trade Pages by Category

- Local buy sell sites
- Garage sale sites

Local Classifieds

Every community has its own places that the locals have adopted. You may already know of the ones in your community but you can also ask around for more ideas. Here's a list of places I'd start:

- CraigsList
- Newspaper Classified (online and in print)
- Facebook Buy/Sell/Trade Pages by Community
- Trade Publications, like *Homes & Lifestyle, AutoTrader, Farm Publications and more!*

Garage/Yard Sales

There can be a gold mine of product virtually right around the corner. There are people that go around to yard sales and garage sales, buy up a lot of things that are underpriced and bring them home to have their own yard or garage sale. This can be very profitable if you get to some of these sales early. Remember the sellers' mentality in my earlier write up. Also another very good trick is to go to these sales at the end of the day. If you offer to haul away what is left or make a low priced offer for all that is left, the seller will usually just want to get rid of it. You could end up with a lot of product for free or almost free to start your own enterprise.

Flea Markets

Flea Markets can be located indoors, or outdoors. If you plan on selling in the flea market system you made need to spend some money on stands and shelters. A good way to test the waters if you are interested in trying this market is to attend one and look for someone with a booth that is not full to the rafters with stock and offer to share the booth and split the cost.

Roadside Markets

One opportunity I have seen, that would be viable in almost any location is a Roadside Market. I have not personally tried this, but you could consider it as a quick way to get into the buy/sell game with little-to-no cash. Yes I said it again: *no cash.* If you have local growers with stands at the front of their properties selling their produce, baked goods, or what have you, there may be an opportunity for you.

I saw a guy parked by a main traffic area the other day selling firewood. There are several campgrounds in close proximity and he left with an empty truck after a couple of hours. I don't know if he cut his own wood, if he bought it or got it on consignment from a friend or commercial woodcutter. Either way it shows that with a little imagination you can find a lot of different items to sell.

I've also frequently seen a pickup truck with a freezer in the back. He parks in our Florida neighborhood and sells fresh seafood. He does pretty well from what I can see. I also saw a guy with a big smoker on a trailer selling smoked ribs and chicken. He must move around to several locations because I only see him once a week. Perhaps he only works part time.

In your travels keep an eye out for roadside vendors. I am sure there are many more viable ideas out there. If you see a good one or dream up a good one let me know and I will post it on our website.

Tip: Before selling anything, especially fresh food on the street, make sure there are no local laws or ordinances you are breaking. You may need a special permit.

If you can get set up in the right location you could make a killing. I know I can't drive by a fresh vegetable stand without stopping and I don't mind paying a higher cost to get something that's farm fresh. The cost of setting this up could be as little as buying three $40 tables and making a homemade sign. (Be sure to check local laws. You may need a vendor's permit and you may have to pay lot rent.)

Tip: The most important factor to consider for a Roadside Market is location. You need a high traffic area with a safe place for traffic to pull into conveniently. Family members could take turns manning the stand and you would only need to be open at peak traffic times.

There are other products that can be sold roadside. The other day I saw a fellow selling throw rugs. He had them draped on stands and there were three or four people looking at them when I drove by. I see hot dog vendors quite often. The opportunities are unlimited, just keep your eyes peeled and you will find plenty of opportunities.

Once you establish a market and a clientele you could possibly import products in the off-season. There you have it, a business in a box.

For a list of good books to read on selling, visit our
Up Your Income Resource page at
www.upyourincomeclub.com/resources

CHAPTER 9

CONSIGNMENT SALES

Consignment Sales are arrangements you make to sell your items through someone else for a fee. They can be a very good way of using someone else's location, marketplace, and customer base to your advantage. Of course, whoever you consign with has to be making some money on the transaction or they won't want to bother. I have consigned many things over the years. If you give an item to a professional that knows the particular market and has the connections, your chances of selling the item are increased greatly.

This leads to another one of my favorite mantras:

Don't worry about what the other guy is making; just worry about what you are making!

If you consign something for $1000 and see that he is asking $2000 you have to realize that there are a lot of factors at play. His cost of marketing, advertising, possible comebacks and warranty costs are all a factor. The market value may well be in the $2000 range. Another consideration is if he pays his staff a commission or if he may have to take a trade and over-allow for it.

In a lot of cases you can let them know what you have for sale without putting it in their store. If you are doing this make sure that you supply them with enough information to effectively do the sale. Give them an accurate description – I do mean *accurate*. Pictures and a complete list of details is a must. Let them know about any flaws. If you mislead the seller and he in turn misleads his customer you will be burning a bridge for life. He will never ever have anything to do with you again. If you are going to continuously use this method you need to cultivate a relationship built on trust and respect.

There are people that just buy items and drop them off at various places for sale. They move them around regularly. One man's aged inventory can be another man's fresh inventory. When something new comes in the sales staff get excited and starts working on it. If, after a few weeks, it is still around, they tend to lose interest. This is just human nature at work. We are all the same.

If you are not into internet marketing you can find people who will list things for sale for you for a few dollars. For example, you may have a family friend who is active on eBay and has a good seller rating. You can also offer what is called a bird dog fee to someone that puts you in contact with a buyer or gives you a good tip on where to sell something.

Some local car lots take consignments too. It's a good idea to research this path before you buy a car for resale. They can tell you pretty close what they can get for the car and what they can pay you. If you can take the vehicle there, ask them for an offer. A lot of car lots make outright purchases. People don't realize that a used car lot buys 90 percent of their inventory. They don't sell new so they don't get the trade-ins the new dealers get. Most of their inventory is usually bought at auction but they also buy off the street or from brokers.

If nothing else the dealer will help you determine a good purchase price. In any case, make sure you determine a value before investing a lot of time and effort into an overpriced item that can't make you any money. Don't be afraid to go back to the seller and show him your research and ask him to adjust his price…before you buy, of course.

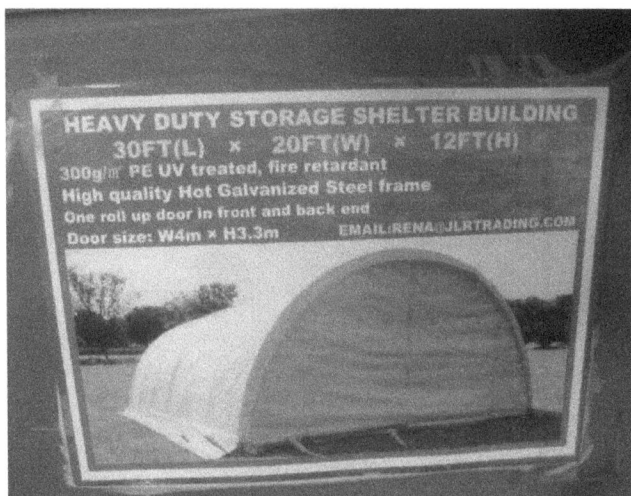

I bought several of these steel frame storage shelters at a disposal sale. I paid $750 each and sold them for them for $1900 to $2400 each. Best of all, I never touched them

PROMOTION

How to market and sell the stuff you buy.

CHAPTER 10

WHY YOUR STUFF ISN'T SELLING

Before you can sell, let's look at why something doesn't sell. There are generally four reasons why a product doesn't sell.

1. Lack of marketing

I have another saying that's relevant here:

If you keep it a secret, you will never sell it.

You have to let as many people as possible know that your product is for sale. (This has to become a part of your mentality if you are going to be successful in the buy/sell game.) Your mind has to automatically kick into marketing mode. Always think about exposing your item to as many interested buyers as you can to sell it as fast as you can.

The internet is a very powerful marketing tool. Craigslist, Kijiijii (in Canada), eBay, local free listings, and many other buy/sell sites can help you get your product out there. Flea markets, garage sales, swap meets. yard sales, auction sales, consignments, street signs, small ads in classifieds, e-mail, Facebook/Twitter (let your friends know), local postings on bill boards, church bulletin boards, are just some other methods of marketing. If it is a bigger item, try and display it in a high traffic area. If you buy at the right price you could possibly sell it to a pawnshop or a shop that sells used items.

One of the easiest places to market is eBay. At the click of a button you can search "For Sale" listings for almost anything. For existing listings, you can get ideas on price and great ways to write your own ads. You can also tell the interest level for an item by the number of views similar items are getting.

Let's say you have a '99 Chevrolet ½-ton pickup for sale. You look one up on eBay and see that it has had an average of 400 views per day. (They usually show how many views the listing has had on the bottom of the page.) You can also see how long the listing has been posted and average out the views per day. If it has been up for 6 days and has 1200 views, it shows you that 200 people per day have at least a passing interest in looking at the truck. If you have the truck in your driveway with a for sale sign, how many people do you think would stop by to browse?

Don't get me wrong I have sold plenty of things from my driveway. I just want to point out the advantage of the internet and show that the more people you can expose your product to, the better. You only need one buyer. If the right person sees it in your driveway, your buyer could literally be just around the corner.

Example: If you are selling a sports car with a lot of modifications you will have a lot better luck listing it under Sports Cars or Special Interest Vehicles than you will putting it in a column that says "Cars for Sale". What you are selling will determine the method of marketing.

2. Presentation

If the truck is sitting in the driveway with a flat tire and all covered in dust and tree sap there is no way anyone is going to buy it. You will notice if you go to any car lot that their vehicles are detailed to the nines. Appearance sells.

Example: Let's say you are looking for a cheap car. You have $1500 to spend. You would like to buy a Buick Century. Your neighbor has one and has had good service out of it. You see two 1999 models advertised. One is priced at $1499 and the other is priced at $999. You go to look at the cars. The one for $999 is in a backyard with a garden hose on the hood. There is tree sap on it, two tires are low. The interior is in excellent condition except for the garbage inside and the ashtray is full. The car starts and runs fine and only has 78,000 miles on it. If you buy it you will have to move some stuff to get it out of there.

The second one you look at is in a garage. He starts it up and backs it out. It runs like a charm. You can see that it has just had a super cleanup. Everything shines. The car has some flaws, it is in similar condition to the first one, and this one has 93,000 miles on it. Nine out of ten people would buy the second one. Most of them won't even bother looking at the first one, they will go with their first impression. I would buy the first one and make it into the second one. With the lower miles I could possibly get $1699 with the right presentation. Do you see how important the presentation is?

Presentation can be applied to just about anything, not just cars. Even an old horse – comb the burrs out of his mane, clip his hooves and shine his coat and he will sell sooner than if he is left as is. This is an important lesson. It is called "Detail for Retail".

There are literally hundreds of methods you can use. The most important factor to consider is your cost of marketing. You'll want to factor the cost of improvements and your marketing costs into your total investment.

3. Price

You will notice that I didn't put price as the number one reason that an item doesn't sell. If you market and present the item properly, you can get more money for it. The price needs to be in the ballpark, but people will pay more for the eye appeal and the presentation. You will increase your odds tremendously if you have a good-looking product.

In the earlier section on the Psychology of a Seller, I show you why in most cases you will be able to get the price adjusted to where you can make some money for your trouble.

Presentation affects price. You see in the example above how the two cars compared price wise and why you can get a lot more money for something just by enhancing the appearance.

If you are going to try to sell an item for your neighbor you need to get the price down to where you can make some money. If he has already had it for sale for a while there could be several reasons that it did not sell. Perhaps he didn't advertise properly, perhaps his price is too high, perhaps the item needs detailing.

If you are going to do something to enhance the appearance you need to be sure that he is willing to compensate you. If it is a vehicle by far the best money you can spend is to take it to a detail shop. They charge between $100 and $200 and you won't recognize the vehicle when it comes out. Before you leap into action get together with him and determine a workable price that will assure you can make some money.

4: Location

Location also affects the desirablity of an item. People in Florida aren't looking for snowblowers – but people who live where it snows frequently will be. Use common sense and always remember the supply and demand rule. Don't waste time and money trying to sell where there's little-to-no demand.

Example: If you are going to use my bicycle example, you will probably have better luck if you are trying to sell used bikes in a poorer community; or a community with lots of children than you are likely to sell on Park Avenue. Park Avenue is where you are more likely to find a bicycle out on the street with the trash, or an expensive bicycle for sale cheap at a garage sale or yard sale.

If it's a vehicle you're selling, you may or may not be able to do much about the location depending on whether or not the vehicle is licensed. If it is you could move it onto a vacant lot in a high traffic area with a sign and a phone number.

The same emphasis on location goes for where you'll place your advertising, you need to use common sense and make sure you place ads where they will be most effective. Your ads also need to be cost effective; spending $20 to place an ad for a bicycle that you are only going to make $30 on doesn't make economic sense.

CHAPTER 11

CAN I MAKE MONEY ON IT?

There are many ways to research and then determine what your selling price should be. Obviously you first need to remember what you bought it for. Then you want to add in your overhead costs, which we will talk about a little later.

Call a friend. Many times when I am not sure of the value of an item I will call someone I know that's very familiar with the item and ask them for an approximate value. They can also tell you about what to watch for, such as an inherent problem: he/she may say; stay away from that type of computer because they have poor memory and tend to lock up regularly and there is no way of fixing them without sending it away, it will cost you more than it is worth. They can also tell you if there is a good market or if it is a dog. They may also be able to tell you the best way to sell it or may actually have a buyer looking for a similar item.

Tip: Establish a network of knowledgeable friends so you can learn about different product categories.

Check local ads or do a search on the computer. If in doubt, run an ad in the local paper, post it online, put up a bulletin, or talk to a friend that might be interested or ask if they know someone that is looking for a similar item. There are many other methods listed throughout this book so I am going to move on and try not to bore you with repetition.

If you specialize in one or two items you will soon get to know the pricing, value, and the upside and downside of each product. You will also find the best places to buy, as well as the best methods to market the product. There are many links on the Resource Page that can help you determine prices.

Determine Your Selling Price Before You Buy

Before you ever buy anything, it is important to know how much you can sell it for. The single most important thing you can do is determine the selling price before you buy. Obviously you have to buy it for less than you can sell it for.

I used to think that I have bought and sold more different types of items than most people on earth, until I visited a pawnshop. They truly deal in just about everything. You need to visit a few to see just how diversified their market is. They can be an excellent resource for determining values and also a good place to sell to. They always have cash at the ready. You need to realize though that if they are paying you $100 then the item is worth a lot more. If you are making money and moving a product quickly there is nothing wrong with selling to them.

Remember, don't worry what the next guy is making, and just worry what you are making.

Depending on what the item is, you may see it for sale at flea markets, swap meets, pawnshops, etc. If you go into a pawnshop and ask a theoretical question such as, "Hi I'm thinking about selling my rifle. It is a Savage lever action 308 caliber in above average condition. It is 8 years old and has only fired about three cases of shells. There are no scratches and it has always been kept in a case. If I brought it in how much would you pay me for it?" He will reply with an outright, "I am not interested" or he will say, "Yeah we buy a lot of guns, if you bring the gun in and it is what you say it is I will give you $X for it." Bingo! You have determined a value and gotten an offer. If you can buy it for less try and sell it for more on your own, try that first; but keep the pawnshop offer as a backup plan.

Many times it may be prudent to advertise an item before you buy it especially if you know it is not going anywhere and will not be sold before you have a chance to market it. This will help you determine if there is any demand for that particular product. Don't forget that the more places you post it and the more people you make aware of it the better the odds are of selling it.

If you get a few calls your odds are pretty good that you will sell it for more. If you get no response sell it to the pawnshop for a quick buck and move on to the next item. Fast money is good money. Cash is King!

My Favorite Website for Research

The internet is the best place to quickly research prices and values on anything so I always recommend you start your research online.

Even if you know nothing about the internet or you don't have a computer, you can and must do some of your research (and sales) this way. Call a friend or hire someone local who can help you. Check your local library to see if they offer classes or help as well. Most libraries also have computers available for free internet access. It won't take very many visits to a site for you to begin to learn how it works and where to find the information you need. Start with one, and then grow your list as you become more comfortable. You can even find books at the library on using the most popular sites.

Example: you work at a tire shop close to three major auto dealerships. The dealerships know that you sell custom wheels and tires so they send you customers that want to upgrade to oversized tires with fancy wheels. Your store is piled up with the takeoffs from the new vehicles and you wonder how to get rid of them because you can only sell so many locally. You search eBay under automotive parts, wheels or tires. You will see plenty for sale. You notice there are two or three predominant sellers. They are selling similar sets of takeoffs to what you need to sell.

By clicking on the seller information you can learn a few things. Number one is the price they are selling for, how long the seller has been selling on eBay, how many sales he has made, and it even shows the satisfaction level of the purchasers. This will show that you can list and sell these all over the country and at what price.

If the storeowner is not taking the trade-ins you could offer to sell them for the customer on a consignment basis and use the same methods. You may want to okay it with your boss so you still have a job to go to.

Overhead Costs

You need to understand what overhead is and how it can effect whether or not you are making any money or just turning your money. (I call it spinning your wheels). When you start out small there will be very few things that will affect your profit.

Advertising, storage, and freight will probably be your biggest cost. Let's say you buy a boat off of eBay in the next city 50 miles away. You get it for one hell of a deal. We will use the same numbers as the boat you got from your neighbor, let's assume this is an identical boat. You bid and you get it for $1000 now you need to go and get it. You pull out the old pickup truck. You fill it up for $120. You take a day off from work because you have to get it out of there within two days and you bought it on a Monday. You get there and find out it has the wrong trailer plug for your truck. You go to a parts store and get an adaptor. There is no spare and one tire doesn't look like it will make it home so you pick up a rim and tire at Walmart. You get the boat home and find out the battery is dead and won't take a charge. You get a battery, clean up the boat, and advertise it for sale.

Here is a breakdown of your overhead:

Fuel $120.00

Work day income lost .... $12.00 x 8hr = 96.00

Meals on the road – you take a friend
(Beers aren't expensed) 36.00

Plug in adapter 12.00

Spare tire and rim from Walmart 80.00

New Battery 69.00

Ad in a local paper 20.00

Cleaning supplies (wax, carwash, etc) 18.00

Your actual cost of the boat is not $1000 like you thought, it is actually $1451. It is amazing how quickly the costs escalate. This is a normal part of the buy and sell game. You will always have additional costs. As long as you realize your costs and come out with a reasonable profit you will be just fine. If you sold the boat for $1900 you would still make $449. Not bad for a day's work. I'll take one of those every day.

Get paid to use your purchases. I bought this two-year-old trailer for $1900 at an auction, then I used it to move some stuff and sold it 3 months later for $3500.

CHAPTER 12

MY SUCCESS & FAILURE LESSONS

Over a period of time, you'll discover that you buy and sell a wide variety of things, but you'll also discover your most profitable niches.

I'm about to share the list of things I've bought and sold over the years, not to brag, but to show you that virtually everything and anything can be bought and sold – and sometimes a novel approach can make you a lot of money.

I once had 6 horses to sell but I figured out a way to sell a total of 48 horses instead; 42 of them were not mine but I made money off of every one of them.

In another case, I bought a truck, hooked it to a trailer and turned around and sold it as a business for a lot more than the truck and trailer were worth individually. I called it "A business in a box."

Another time, I bought a brand new house at auction for $189,000; it is now rented and netting $1100 per month and I don't have one penny of my own money invested in it.

There are many stories on a lower scale that were done when I had no funds. They are probably the most innovative.

Here are some of the items that I have bought and sold:

- Bicycles
- Cars and Trucks
- Highway Tractors (I don't even have a license to drive one!)
- Wrecked cars and trucks (salvage) Sold "as is"
- Used lawn mowers
- Antiques
- Horses and Cows
- Airplanes
- Silverware (for the metal value)
- Real Estate
- Skid steers
- Mobile homes
- Houses for removal
- Motorcycles
- Snowmobiles
- Watercraft
- Boats
- Hot tubs (Trailer Load)
- Massage chairs, (trailer load)
- Campers
- Trailers- from small utility to semi trailers

- Street sweepers
- Fence posts
- Wheels and tires
- Tools
- New Hydrostatic Noma riding mowers (trailer load)

I keep thinking of more but will stop here. I'm sure I'll share more in our Facebook group and I invite you to do the same. The funniest one is the story about fence posts. But I digress...

Avoiding Costly Lessons

To show you how sometimes an item can be absolutely stolen at an auction, I am going to tell you about a loss that I took and one of the most expensive lessons I've ever learned. You're about to discover how it happened, and why so you don't let it happen to you. You'll also discover how it can work to your advantage, like it did for my buyer.

In 2012, I bought a 2005 Johnson street sweeper on eBay for $15,000. It had low miles and was in very good condition. New replacement, I would say, was in the $120,000+ range.

I have sold sweepers in the past and done well with them, but admittedly I am getting old and lazy. Making a long story short; I didn't follow my own marketing guidelines and never even got around to advertising the sweeper except in the local Auto Trader.

I have no excuse other than I am getting complacent in my old age and didn't get around to doing a creditable marketing job.

At this time, with freight, my investment into the sweeper was about $18,000. After 'sitting on it' for a while,(2 years) I decided to ship it to Ritchie Brothers Auction. I saw a similar sweeper sell in Florida for around $17,000 that wasn't anywhere near the condition that mine was in. I knew that by the time I paid the auction commissions, and the freight, I was probably going to lose a little money, but at this point I was ready to be rid of it.

Oh-boy was I going to lose some money.

Ritchie is a truly an unreserved auction. Everything sells to the highest bidder. My 2005 sweeper sold for $4,750. Right after it, they sold a 1996 sweeper for exactly the same price $4,750. Shows that you can never predict the outcome until the auction is over. Someone got a heck of a deal that day.

I am ashamed of my own laziness and poor judgement, but am telling about it because the story contains several valuable lessons that you need to understand. Let us review the situation:

Lesson #1: Market it.

I, of all people, should know better than to buy an expensive item and then not do the marketing. I call this passive marketing. Another term is Lazy Daze marketing. I use the word Daze because when you market this way you probably are in a daze. There is no nice way to put it. If you get lazy and complacent you can and will lose money.

Lesson #2: Do everything you can.

When the time came to get rid of the aged unit I could have done several things to get rid of it and still come out okay. I could have followed my own guidelines and listed it to towns and municipalities. I could have sent info to, or called other dealers that market similar products. I could have moved it to a different location and perhaps consigned it. I could have tried it on eBay or Craigslist. Instead I decided to send it to auction, because I was leaving for the winter and just wanted to get rid of it.

Lesson #3: Buy things in demand.

There are bargains everywhere. I had a sweeper to sell but there was no demand. The person that bought the sweeper from me basically won the lottery that day. He was probably not there to buy a sweeper but was smart enough to take advantage of the bargain. Miracles do happen. Hopefully he buys my book so that he can learn how to sell it for the money I should have gotten for it.

Lesson #4: Don't wait too long.

Yes, you need to move your aged inventory, but you don't and shouldn't have to give away the farm to do it. Start working on getting rid of it long before it becomes a problem. If it is a problem don't let yourself lose interest like I did.

Lesson #5: Sell it in season.

I sold the sweeper in the fall and should have held it until spring. The sweeper would have more value in the spring as I live in the Snow Belt. Amazing how many lessons can be made from a $15,000 loss. Don't try this at home.

Okay, I told you where to buy things and where to sell things. Now let's talk about how to write killer ads.

CHAPTER 13

HOW TO WRITE ADS LIKE A PRO

Learning to write a great ad is a skill you should acquire as soon as possible. As we've already discussed, the more detail you can put into an ad, the better. That reduces surprises and strengthens your position as an honest seller.

Always, always, always, tell the truth. Never misrepresent your product. Sure you have to make it sound as good as possible, and you maybe won't mention the small paint touch up you did, but always tell the truth. You will gain more trust from your buyer and find it much easier to sell to him/her if they have decided that you are forthcoming and honest.

If the buyer calls or e-mails and asks you to describe your product, do so as accurately as possible. Basically describe what they will see when they come. There is an old saying in the selling business. "Tell it like it is not like it should be". If you tell your buyer about some flaws that he is going to see anyway, you accomplish two things.

1. You build trust.
2. You remove objections to the price.

For example if you didn't tell him about a couple of scratches and a small dent, he can say, you told me this thing is perfect and look at these scratches and this dent. If you had handled the description properly there would be no problem. The buyer knows that used items have imperfections and if the scratches and dent were a problem to him then he wouldn't have come and you wouldn't be wasting both of your time.

Where you advertise and how much it costs will determine the size of your ad. If it is a free listing with lots of room for dialog, by all means give as much important information as possible. Notice I said important. Don't go on and on about irrelevant drivel, stick to the point.

The best way to write an ad is by asking yourself the five things a buyer would ask and then answer the questions in the ad.

Always make sure your ad stands out from the rest, don't follow the flow of humdrum ads.

Example: Typical ad under the heading- Bicycle for sale:

For sale: Men's bike 20 in tires, good condition.
$80 OBO (or best offer)

Your ad:

Men's bike 20in tires, 8 speed, shines like new, used very little, pictures available, excellent tires, you won't find a nicer one.
Replacement cost $360.
$100 OBO

If you had to drive to look at one, which one would you go and see?

Of course this statement needs to be true. If the bike is faded and the tires are worn out you should have bought it for $10 or got it for free and be selling it for $30 or $40 and your ad should say:

Men's bike 20in tires, 8 speed
Needs a little TLC - $45 OBO

Or shine it up and put some cheap tires on it and sell it for a lot more. Believe it or not there are a lot of buyers that are looking for things that need work that they can save a buck on. If you tell the truth you will save a lot of aggravation. I made a lot of money over the years buying wrecked cars from insurance companies and reselling them (as is) to be repaired.

There is an art to writing ads. On the *Up Your Income* Resources page I share a link to my favorite book that has knockout ads where you virtually just fill in the blanks.

Now on to the money stuff.

MONEY MATTERS

Dealing with the money aspect of your new business.

CHAPTER 14

HOW MUCH CASH HAVE YOU GOT?

Way back in the beginning of the book, we talked about how you can start your business with little or no money. Remember you need to be patient when it comes to your money, don't spend it as soon as you get it.

Before you buy your first item, you need to determine how much cash you have to spend. Be sensible, don't spend all the rent. Also remember that it might take a little time before the item you buy sells and you get your initial investment back.

Let's say you have $100. You are in good shape. I am going to create a scenario to show you how quickly your money can grow. This is not based on anything I have done recently but is what I could do if I landed back on earth with just $100. Remember: You can start with a lot less.

Let's use bikes for our first example. Bikes are a good place to start if you have very little money. Although, if you have more money to start with you can use these same methods for almost anything.

To begin, I would learn a bit about bikes before I went picking so I knew the difference between a desirable bike and an undesirable bike. If you have a kid in your family that is into bikes, it might be a good idea to take him along. Go to a used bike shop and check out the models and the prices.

After I was familiar with the market, I would go to an auction and buy a few bikes, trikes, wagons, etc. for $10 to $30 each. A police or city auction will probably have the biggest selection.

Tip: If you are intimidated by auctions try the local paper/ bargain hunter, etc. Garage sales, or yard sales are also a good source that is close to home. Also, a lot of newspapers and selling sites have a free or to give away section.

I would put the bikes I bought on my lawn with a "For Sale" sign, I would list them in free local buy/sell magazines, I would put them online, I would put up posters on local free bill boards and I would offer the kids on my block a finder's fee if they know of someone looking for a bike. If I had the time, I could set up on a vacant lot in a high traffic area - with one or two bikes and a "For Sale" sign. (This should keep you under the radar of neighborhood by-laws.)

Your profit is always made when you buy; don't get caught up in the emotion of buying. Set a price ahead of time and stick to it.

I'll give you a good example of why you want to know the value of something before you buy for resale. Recently, my wife and I went to a flea market to look for an electric miter saw. I wasn't looking for one for resale. I needed one for a project in my home. I assumed that tools would obviously be a lot cheaper there. I found one hell of a deal on a 10-inch saw. The guy was asking only $80 which I thought was reasonable because the saw only looked like it had been used a couple of times and was still in the box it came in.

I offered him $70 which he took with great reluctance letting me know he was barely recovering his cost. On the way home I stopped at a Sears's clearance center to confirm my great deal. I saw a very similar saw for $74.95 brand new. Later that week another store had the exact same saw on for $64.95 I'm glad I didn't buy it to resell because I would be screwed for any hope of making money. If I had searched the internet for two minutes before I went to the flea market I would have known the market for this product.

I bought this Blazer in Florida for $3500 and sold it in Canada for $10,700. I made a profit of $5,200 after expenses!

CHAPTER 15

THE 80/20 RULE - DON'T BE AFRAID TO LOSE SOMETIMES

Looking back at my successes and failures, one of the best pieces of advice I can give you is to have some sort of idea of when to let go.

Car dealerships have a way of keeping their used car managers from letting their aged inventory become a problem. It is a very simple procedure, they go on a 60- or 90-day limit. All used vehicles have to be disposed of before the 60- or 90-day limit even if they suffer a loss. This keeps the mistakes from being set aside and forgotten about. It is very easy to let your mistakes pile up. This is a problem I have struggled with constantly over the years.

Let's say you are working with $1000 and you buy three items at an average of $333 each. You sell two and have one left. You do the same the next month. You now have $666 tied up in slow moving inventory. You are not in any trouble yet, but, fast forward 6 months $333 x 6 = $1998

Or fast-forward a year $333 x 12 = $3996. You can see where the dead inventory can slowly eat up your operating capital. That is why the 80/20 theory has worked for me. Basically what I am saying is don't be afraid to lose once in a while. If you win on 80 percent and lose on 20 percent you will do just fine.

I have another saying that applies to this same rule:

"Sell it for what it is worth!"

In other words if you bought it for $500 and you know it is worth $1000 then don't sell it for $700. In the same breath, if you have had the item for a couple of months and the feedback is that you are asking too much and you realize your odds of selling it are diminishing, then sell it for $400 if that is what it is truly worth.

There is no shame in making a mistake as long as you learn from it and don't keep making the same mistake. Your first loss is usually your best loss. In other words if you get an offer that is close to the value, don't play games, let it go and go out and spend the money on something that can make it up. It is important to make your money work for you. As you build your money and have more pieces in inventory this will become increasingly difficult. I know I have more than $100,000 in aged inventory right now and after reading my own advice I am going to smarten up and get rid of it.

The best way to learn is by hearing about the success and failures of other people who buy and sell for profit. Be sure to join and engage in our free Picker's Club on Facebook at
www.Facebook.com/groups/pickersclub

CHAPTER 16

CONTROLLING YOUR INVENTORY

This is something I have struggled with throughout my buying and selling career. At first when you don't have a lot of money to work with you will put in a lot more effort to get rid of an item that just won't go away.

Remember the 80/20 rule? So what if you lose on the odd one, as long as you win most of the time. I have years of experience and still end up with mistakes that won't go away. My problem has been to discipline myself to concentrate on getting rid of them. I tend to lose interest and just let them sit. This happens because I am turning enough money that it doesn't slow me down much, but it is the absolute wrong way to do business.

There is also such a thing as too much inventory. You won't have this problem when you first start, but trust me it will eventually creep up on you if you don't keep your finger on the pulse of what you are doing. A good way is to have a 60- or 90-day policy just like car dealers do. When the clock hits the pre-agreed time limit you have to get rid of it. Please take this seriously because it will have a profound influence on how quickly you build your fortune. This will make you get creative in your marketing and perhaps you will learn a newer, better way of marketing.

I'll tell you a story about how I learned a valuable marketing lesson from an aged piece of inventory. A few years back I was at an auction (story of my life). I noticed a one-ton garbage truck. It was about ten years old. It was in good condition and I have done well over the years buying oddball stuff. I thought if this thing goes cheap I'm going to buy it. I thought $2500 was where I would like to be, this was my gut feeling of the wholesale value. I had no experience in this market (sometimes you just have to wing it). I bought the truck at the auction for $1400.

This is where it gets interesting. I brought the truck home and put it on my lot in my hometown of 800 people. Don't know why but none of the 800 seemed very interested. I advertised it in the local paper as well as the nearest city paper and of course in the *Auto Trader*. (The internet was not yet available).

Nothing. Not one call.

In the mean time I sure got a ribbing from the locals. "What are you going into the garbage business? Are you a garbage man now? What days do you want me to put out my garbage…" I'll stop now but there were many more ribbings I can assure you. They were all in good fun and made me twice as determined to sell the truck.

After about three months with not one inquiry, I knew I had to take the truck back to the auction and admit defeat, or find a different way of marketing my product. By now the locals were having a lot of fun with me.

I was on the town council at the time. While attending a meeting I noticed a newsletter on the administrator's desk. It was a municipal newsletter that went out to all of the small towns and rural municipalities.

I thumbed through it and noticed some equipment ads on the back page. You guessed it. A light came out of the fog. What if I were to advertise my garbage truck to the towns and rural municipalities or counties? I placed an ad and waited. Within a few days of the ad coming out I had action. Lots of action! It appears that I didn't know where to sell a garbage truck and these people didn't know where to buy a garbage truck. It was a match made in heaven.

I sold the truck for $4200.

I gave you an example earlier in the book showing what a strong effect inventory control can have on your overall business outcome. Oh yeah! Did I forget to mention that this is a business?

Sure when you first get started and are selling one or two pieces a month you can consider it to be a hobby. But if you get the bug and start doing some volume, you should consider it to be a business and run it like a business. Keeping a simple set of books and keeping the books up to date will give you control. There are several One Write Systems such as QuickBooks which is what I use. There are many less expensive programs available. I will post links on my site. If you set it up to write your checks on the computer it pretty much automatically keeps your books for you.

Caution! Don't try this at home. This is a photo of my biggest mistake ever! I lost over $15,000 on this street sweeper machine; and I can't blame anyone else!

CHAPTER 17

CREDIT: HOW TO GET IT AND HOW TO USE IT

There are many kinds of credit. You need to understand them and use them to your advantage.

There is bank credit. This is available if you are well established and or have plenty of equity, also they like to see you have a track record in the proposed business. Notice again that I called it a business.

If you are renting your home, have no money and drive a "Buy Here, Pay Here" car, you need to find other ways of getting credit. If you are the person I have just described and you go into a bank and tell them that you need a loan because you are going to start buying and selling for a living, you will have the whole staff rolling around on the floor laughing, probably even some of the customers that happen to be in the bank at the time. Basically it is not going to happen.

If you haven't burnt all your bridges, you can ask a friend for financial help getting started or, once again, starting with consignments (if you are selling something for somebody they are effectively loaning you their item to sell). This is a trust situation and in my eyes is the same as a loan.

One thing you must understand is that whatever method you use to get and use credit you must always pay your loan or credit line back as per your agreement. There is no faster way to lose a friend or creditor than by not paying them or by misleading them or trying to float another deal on the guy's money when you said you would pay him back when you sold this one. If you are not honorable, forthright and trustworthy to a fault you will inevitably fail.

In the buying and selling game your word is your bond. If you are dealing in a certain commodity; (sooner or later you will start to specialize) such as you decide to buy and sell trading cards. You will fairly quickly get to know a lot of people that buy and sell the same thing. It is like a rodeo circuit. If you develop a reputation as a standup guy that is always true to his word you will be able to do deals verbally over the phone or by e-mail because you are a trusted source.

You must become a trusted source if you are continuously selling to the same people. This makes things a lot easier and faster. I have pre-sold many things by simply finding them and making a call to someone I knew they would be interested in a particular item and had them commit over the phone because they knew that it would be exactly as I described it. In a case like this your word is your credit. The seller trusts you to pay him. The buyer trusts you to deliver once he has spoken for it. Everybody is in a trust situation which makes for good business as well as repeat business. It is a binding deal for all three involved.

CHAPTER 18

HOW TO PAY AND GET PAID SECURELY

Getting paid is the best way to avoid going broke! Don't sell anything on credit unless you are in the "Buy Here Pay Here" game. I will explain at the end of this chapter just how this works. Once again, cash is king. You will get many offers to pay for a part of the sale price and pay the rest later.

__Warning:__ If you agree to partial or delayed payment – you're playing with a recipe for disaster, especially in the first part of your career when you are going through your learning curve and trying to build your cash reserves. The only way this can work is if the item stays in your possession and you have clearly laid out terms as to how and when it will be paid out. Don't get into a situation where a buyer ties you up for a long period of time.

Example: You have a car for sale. It is a beater and you are selling it for $1600. A buyer comes along and says, "Gee I really want the car. Can I give you $1000 now and give you the rest next month?" (Hopefully you only have $1000 invested). I would say fine, I will take $1000 down and hold the car for you for a month. If he agrees, make sure you have a clearly written agreement with no doubt as to the terms and have him sign it.

If you give credit you are taking your operating money out of circulation as well as increasing greatly the odds of losing money. There is an old saying in the car business: "A paid-for car runs better than one that has money owing against it." If they owe you money, they keep finding things wrong that they expect you to fix for one of two reasons. One is you are still a co-owner of the car and two, it is a perfect stall tactic to delay payment.

Let us say you have started with nothing and built yourself up to working with $2500 over a period of three months. Instead of selling one $1200 item per month you are selling two. Your nest egg is starting to grow.

If you take a $1200 item and sell it on credit you are taking a huge step backward. You now have half the working capital that you had and have only half the potential to make money. You always need to have a cash reserve so that if a good buy comes along, (they often do) you are ready to pull the trigger.

Always, ALWAYS make sure that the paper work is in order when you are buying and when you are selling.

If you suspect anything wrong about the product stay away from it. The fastest way to get put out of business is to knowingly or unknowingly buy stolen property. Remember you need to build a reputation in your chosen field. There are millions of legitimate places to buy so don't enter the grey area. It may seem like easy money but it never lasts. Insist on cash or cashier's check for items you are selling. If you get a cashier's check from a stranger take him to your nearest bank and cash it before you give him the item. Most people are honest but there are scammers out there. In all cases use common sense.

If you are selling online you can use PayPal. They are a payment exchange service that will do your transaction for a fee. There are others too. Since your options are constantly changing, that's a great thing to ask about in our Facebook group.

Buy Here, Pay Here

I promised to tell you how "Buy Here, Pay Here" works. Basically it is a simple concept that can make a lot of money. I'll give an example of one theoretical deal that will show you how much money they can drag out of one transaction. This story is based on a car deal although I am sure the same principal is used in other businesses.

Example: A dealer buys a car for $1000, brings it home and puts it on his lot for $1999. He puts a sticker in the window for $600 down. You come along and decide to buy the car. You have a job, but have had poor credit in the past. The dealer checks your pay stubs and says you are good to go. He writes up a deal as follows. Taxes will be extra. There may be other fees.

Purchase price $1,999

Documentation fee $369

Total purchase price $2,368

Less down payment .... - $600

Balance owing $1768 to be paid over a 6 month period at 32% per annum interest = $322.77 per month for 6 months.

At the end of six months you will have paid the dealer $2536.62. I haven't included insurance or any other fees that he may charge. The car that he paid $1000 for, and was asking $1999 for will have more than doubled his money. He made a markup of $1536.62. It doesn't take long to build up a substantial inventory at this rate although there are risks involved. Don't try this at home. There is a lot more you need to know about this business if you are thinking of getting into it.

CHAPTER 19

INCOME TAXES: HOW THEY AFFECT YOU

When you first get started and are not doing any volume (or you're buying for personal reasons) you probably don't need to worry much about taxes. There are two taxes that can affect your income as well as your future. If you are in business it is the law to collect sales tax and to pay income tax on your net earnings. Most people don't like to pay tax and feel that if there is a way of avoiding it they will. You need to be aware that this can come back to bite you.

Here's an example of how that can happen: Mary started buying and selling antiques four years ago. In the first year she sold $8400 worth of product. She wrote checks for some of her product and paid cash for the rest. She deposited most of the proceeds into her bank account.

In the second year she had her market figured out and started selling at flea markets and consigning certain special items to an antique storeowner she had gotten to know and trust. In the second year she sold $36,000 worth of product. Again she paid cash for some and wrote checks for the rest. She didn't keep track of her expenses (overhead costs). She wasn't collecting state sales tax and she wasn't claiming any income.

That year the state was doing a tax audit on the antique dealer's books and the auditor noticed quite a few payments made to Mary. The auditor asked about her relationship with the antique dealer and was told that she regularly consigned product for sale. This got her onto a future audit list.

Mary continued merrily on her way and by the time four years rolled around she was selling over $100,000 plus in product. She got a notice that she was being audited. They said they would need all of her income and all of her expenses. "Jeez Louise I didn't keep books, I was too busy!"

The first place an auditor looks is at your bank statement. They can and will get them from your bank if you can't supply them. This is basically a set of books for the revenue people and if you don't keep detailed records they will use this as your primary information. Mary did not have a set of books so the auditor took her statement which showed total deposits over the last four years of $180,000 from her sales proceeds. The state tax is 7 percent so she was immediately assessed for $12,600 plus penalties and interest which totaled about $18,000 which was payable instantly. Wait it gets worse!

The state auditor took his money out of Mary's account and went on his merry way. Of course he passed on the information to his bigger associate, the federal government and four months later Mary got a notice that the Feds would like to take a peek at her books. Mary says what books? The auditor says we'll work with what you've got. He seemed like such a nice guy.

He takes her statements and takes the $180,000 income and deducts the check amounts written for product.

Remember she paid cash for a lot of expenses and did not keep receipts. They found about $90,000 worth of expenses as per the checks written, so assumed Mary had a $90,000 dollar income. The amount owing with penalties and interest came out to $36,000 Mary said, "But wait! I didn't make that kind of money!"

The auditor said, "Don't worry. If you can provide me with receipts and detailed expenses, I can perhaps get it lowered."

Mary said, "But wait! I don't have receipts I paid cash for the flea market booth and for some of the stock."

"Great," said the auditor. "How much do you figure you paid out in cash?"

Mary guesses $50,000 in reply. "We need to lower my income by $50,000" The auditor now replies, "Well then, we have a new problem. Now you have to show me where the $50,000 came from. Unless you borrowed it, got it from your mother, or won it, I will have to add it to your income."

Mary worked hard but she did everything the wrong way. I have said many times in this book that this is a business. If you are going to get into this game full time or even part time you need to do things right. In many cases there are a lot of tax advantages that you can use to lessen the tax burden. You can write off all kinds of expenses if you keep detailed records, even meals, fuel, cell phones, vehicles, and many other things become tax deductible when you are running a legitimate business.

Sales Tax

Always collect and submit sales tax unless you are selling out of state on the internet. There are some "loopholes" they haven't closed yet. Even still, you need detailed records to prove it went out of state. Either shipping reciepts or signed way bills will suffice. Accurate records are a must.

Write Off Expenses

My wife and I have traveled all over Canada and the U.S. and we write off the bulk of our food and travel expenses because we incorporate picking for profit into our adventure. Tax deduction laws vary depending on where you live, but don't miss out on this very big opportunity to get paid to hunt for items in all kinds of cool locations. In many cases, you can also employ your kids and grandkids to help you and write off their paycheck as well. A good accountant can help you establish yourself as a business and help you identify a lot more ways to write off your expenses.

Bookkeepers and Accountants

If you are like me and have an attention deficit problem, then get someone else to do your books. Bookkeepers are worth their weight in gold. I have never spent time on bookkeeping myself. I have always paid someone to do it. I have had about six audits in the last ten or twelve years without any surprises.

If you want to manage your books yourself, be sure you have adequate training and you stay on top of your numbers regularly. Not watching your cashflow is a great way to go broke quickly. In most cases, a good accountant or bookkeeper will pay for themselves by helping you avoid costly mistakes.

CHAPTER 20

IN CONCLUSION...

I want to personally thank you for reading this book. You have taken the first step on a journey that I hope to share with you. Once you have read the book you will know if this lifestyle is for you. If you have decided that you would like to drastically "Up Your Income" by using these methods, join our free private Facebook group. It's called "Pickers Club" It is absolutely free! You can find us at

www.fb.com/groups/pickersclub

This community is a great place to share information, links, and ideas, and to ask questions. You'll also have access to a lot of other perks and opportunities coming your way as a member.

I'll see you in the group!

ABOUT THE AUTHOR

Ladimer Kowalchuk grew up in a small town in rural Canada. Even in his younger years he was always driven by the desire to make more money so he could buy the things he wanted. Ladimer worked part time after school but always hated the fact that he could only make so much money for an hour's work. It didn't seem fair. There had to be a better way.

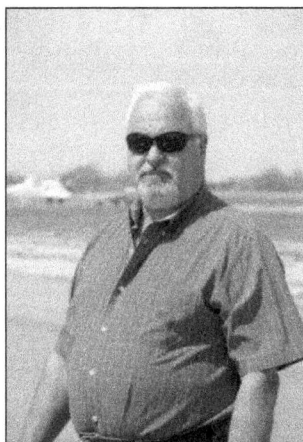

Early in his married life he wanted to buy a bike for his 5-year-old son. He was working for an hourly wage and was broke as usual. He decided to buy a used bike from a neighbor who was having a moving sale. Instead of one bike, the neighbor talked him into buying three used bikes for $50.

He had an "Ah-ha!" moment when he sold two bikes for $50.00 each and kept one for his son. Hooked on the easy profit, he started buying and selling for a side income. Within a few months, he was making a better living, and soon he started buying and selling everything from cars and bikes to household goods and after a few years' even airplanes (excluding the infamous street sweeper mishap).

Ladimer and his wife now enjoy a great lifestyle buying and selling on tax-deductible road trips throughout the US and Canada – and helping others do the same.

You'll find an unending supply of interesting stories, tips, and moneymaking advice, with actual real life examples throughout his book. His favorite saying is, "I trip over more than $100 almost every day."

TESTIMONIALS

"I first met Ladimer 33 years ago. His way of life always intrigued me. I was working at a steady job and having trouble making ends meet. By watching him and following some of the deals he was making I soon realized that I could make some extra money while still holding down a regular job. I eventually was able to leave my job and now own a successful contracting business. I still buy and sell more than a dozen items in an average month and will probably never quit. It has become a way of life."

- Lawrence R., Yorkton Sask, Canada.

"Ladimer is a neighbor and a friend. I have watched him with interest over the years. He has done some very interesting things. You never know what he is going to come home with. I have seen him buy many items which he was always able to resell. He seems to have a knack for recognizing opportunity and for acting on it. I now buy and sell a few things for fun and have made as much as $10,000 on one deal."

- Brad H., Ituna Sask, Canada

"I met Ladimer 3 years ago. I sell items proffesionally on E-Bay for other people as well as for myself. I was stuggling; I live in Florida and the economy was in the tank; Ladimer helped me to recognize several opportunities that were virtually right under my nose. He took the time to show me how to turn my business into a money making enterprize. I am now making decent money and the future looks bright. His methods are easy to follow and I don't hesitate to recommend his system."

- Jose V., Saint Petersburg Fl.

"As long as I have known Ladimer(46 years) he has been involved and intrigued with the concept of making money. He has the gift of turning a profit on almost anything. He has an uncanny ability to understand the concept of doing what most people fear—making a very successful career of buying and selling. I have read Ladimer's book and learned that it is my own fears that stop me. Thank you Ladimer for writing a book that takes the fear out of and gives hope for anyone who wants to make money; either out of a need or just for pleasure".

- Karen W., Houston Texas

www.ingramcontent.com/pod-product-compliance
Lightning Source LLC
Chambersburg PA
CBHW060627210326
41520CB00010B/1498